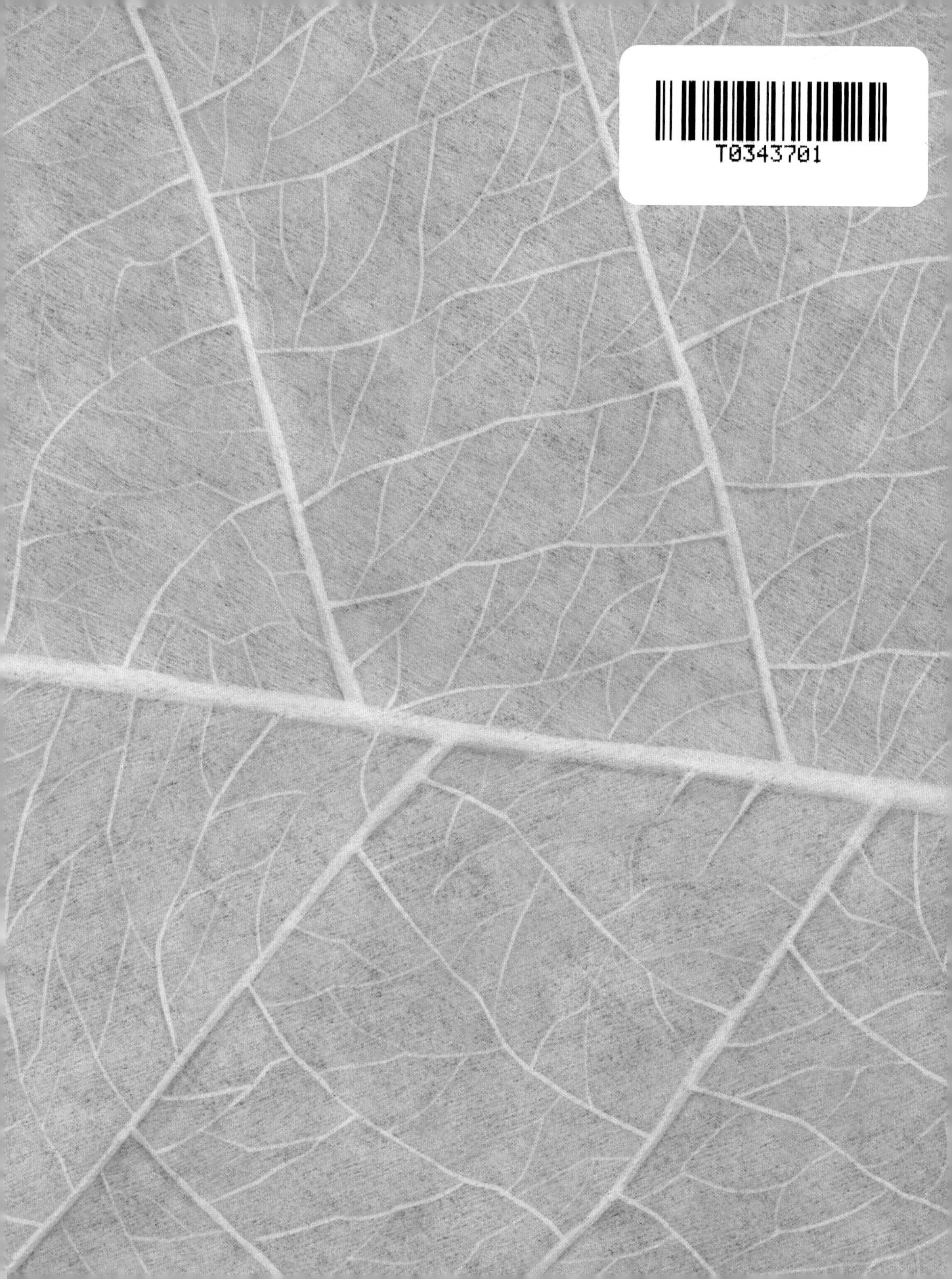

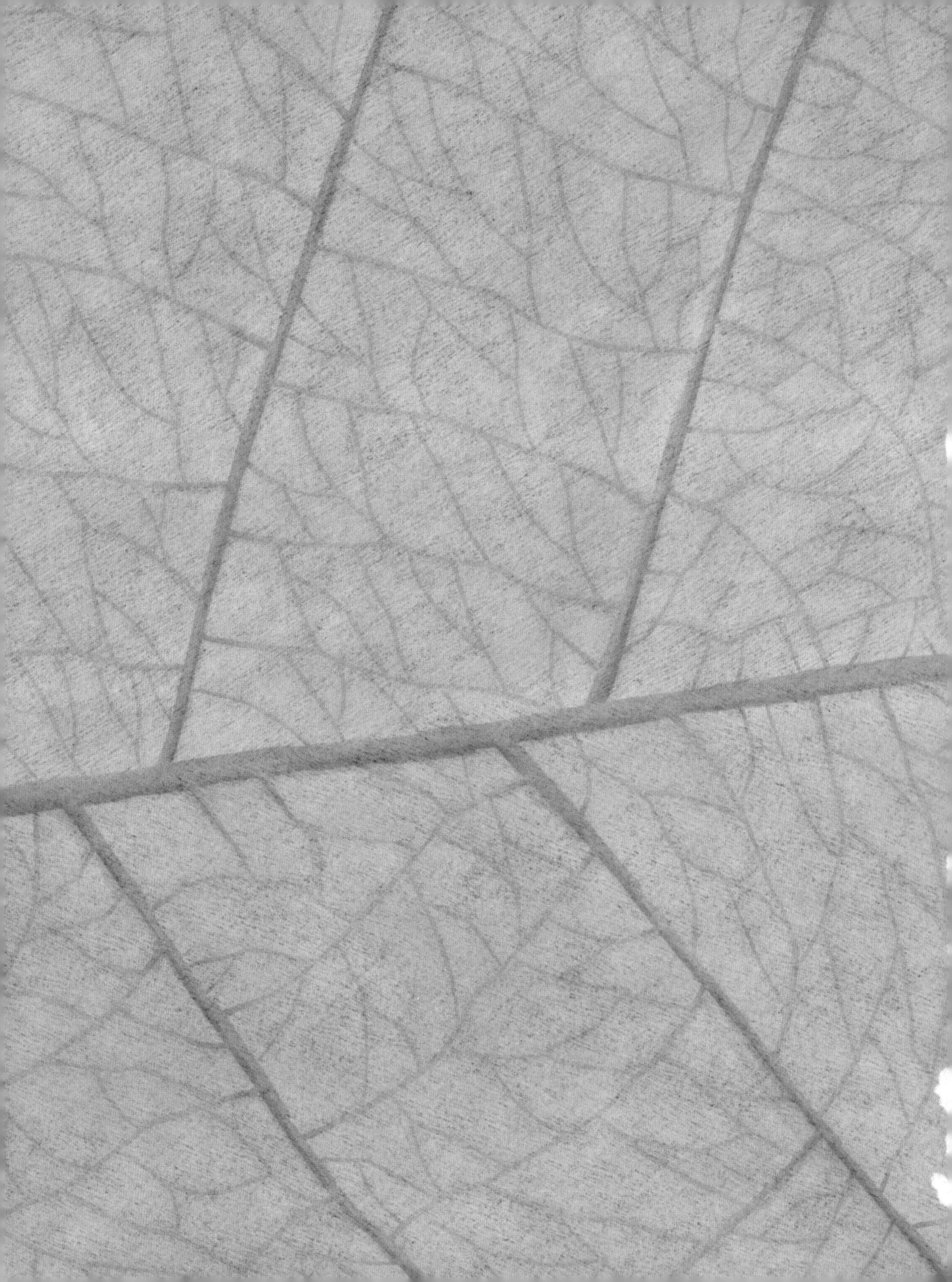

Being Kind

How to add more meaning to your moments

Written by Kobi Yamada
Illustrated by Charles Santoso

Kindness is good for you—it's good for your health and it's good for your spirit. Being kind enhances your resiliency, and makes you calmer and happier. It increases self-confidence, boosts your mood, and inspires personal growth. It brings people closer to you and makes you feel more loved and more loving.

Kindness is not just something you do, but something you are.

Practicing kindness doesn't have to be a grand gesture. Sometimes just a little, seemingly insignificant thing can mean more than you know. A moment of support in a time of need, a quiet word of encouragement, a helping hand, or just a warm smile that says, "I see you," can start a chain reaction of good feelings and kind deeds that brighten everything they touch.

Plot your contribution to the world.
Be part of the day rising to its potential.

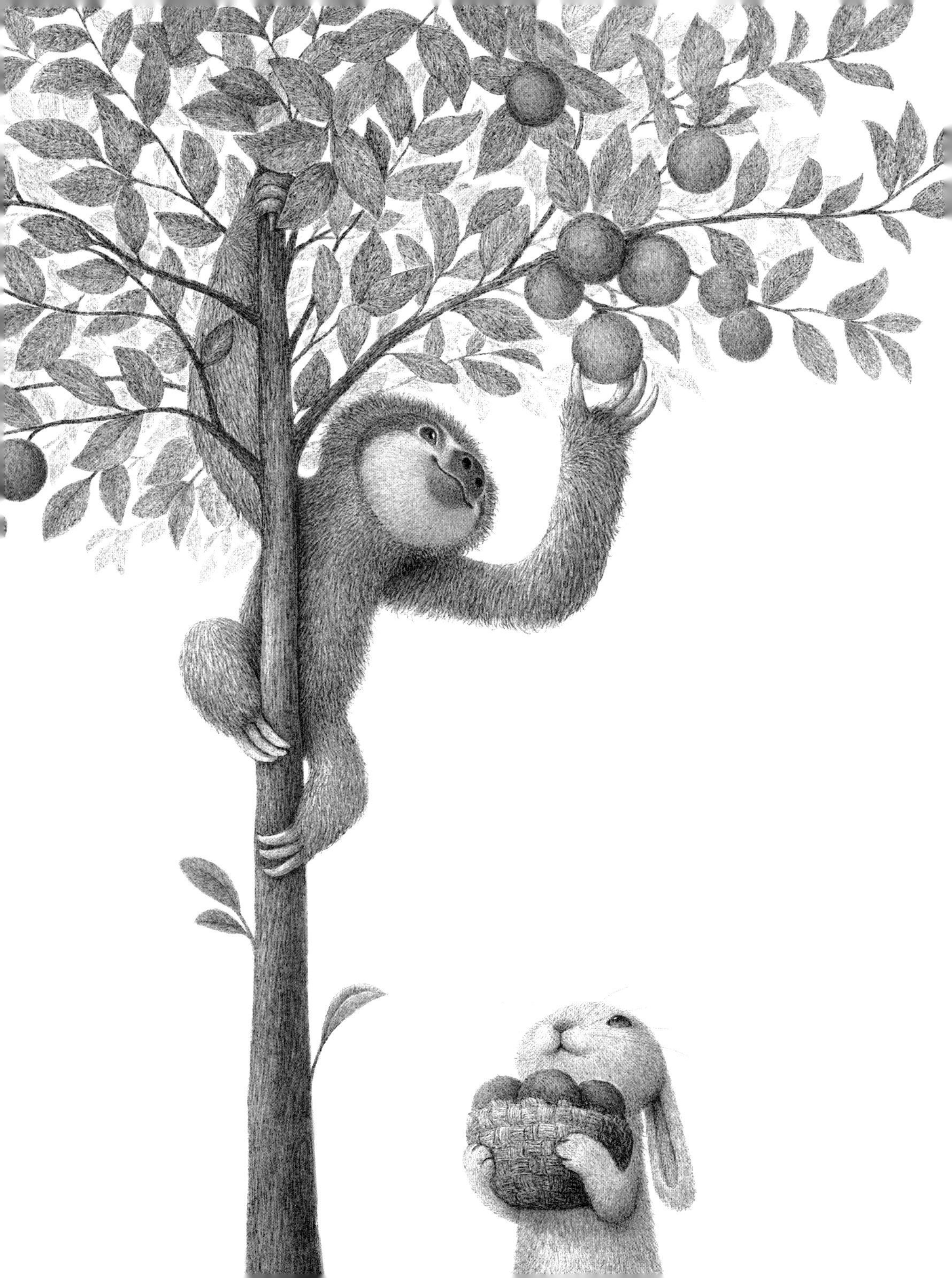

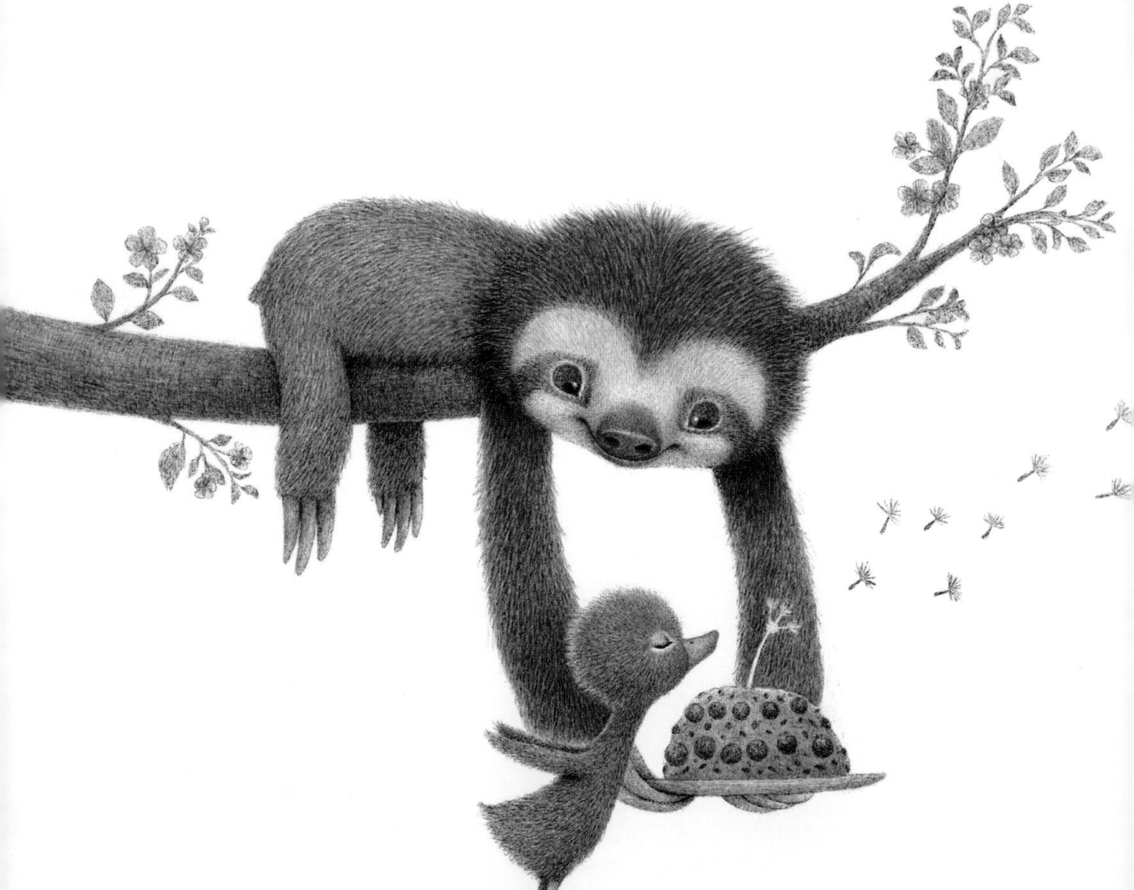

Give freely. You are meant to share your talents
and abilities. That's why they're called gifts.

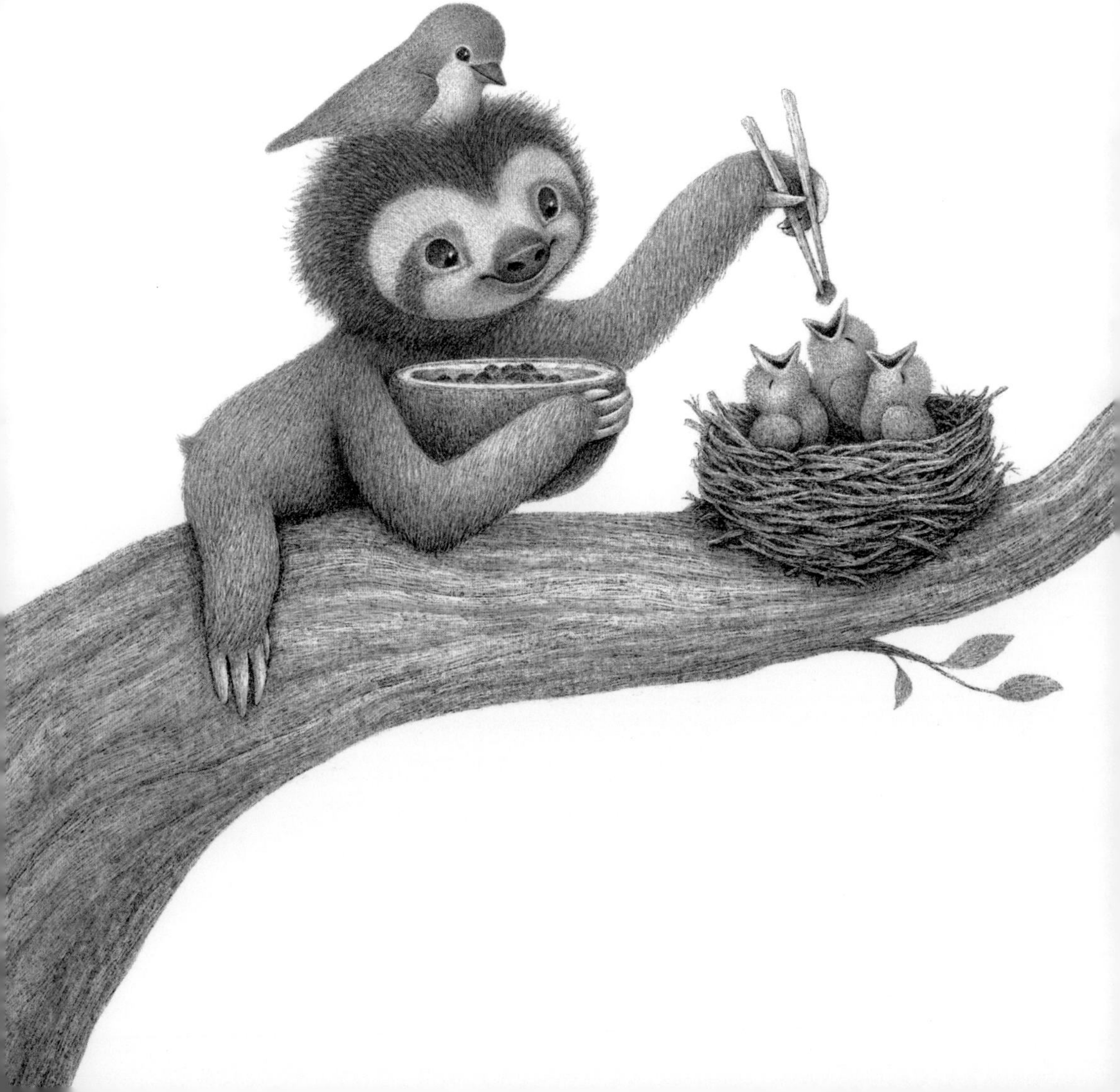

We all have the power to make life a little bit easier for each other.
Let the good you think and feel be the good you do.

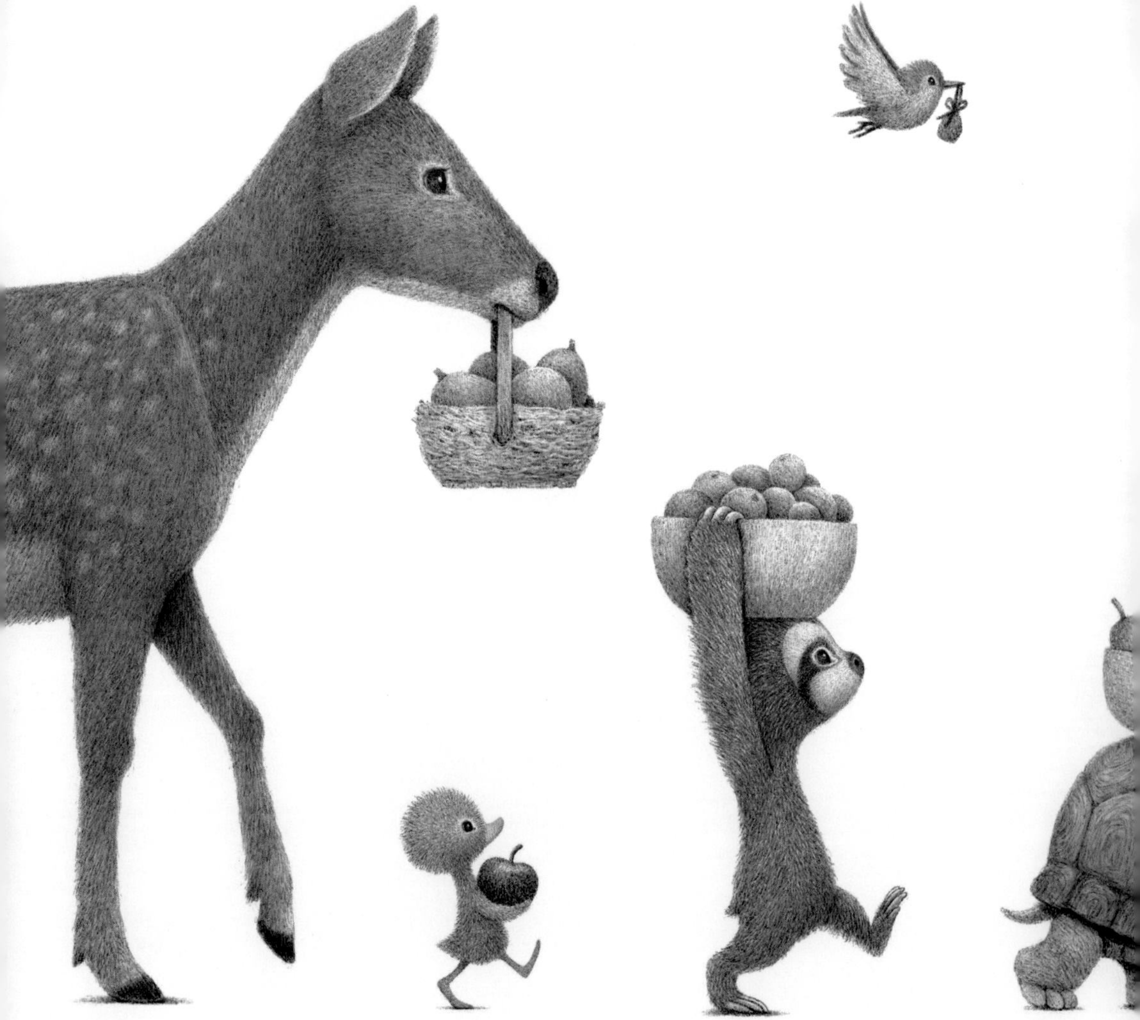

Comparison is the opposite of being kind to yourself and others.
Negativity and positivity increase with use. Choose wisely.

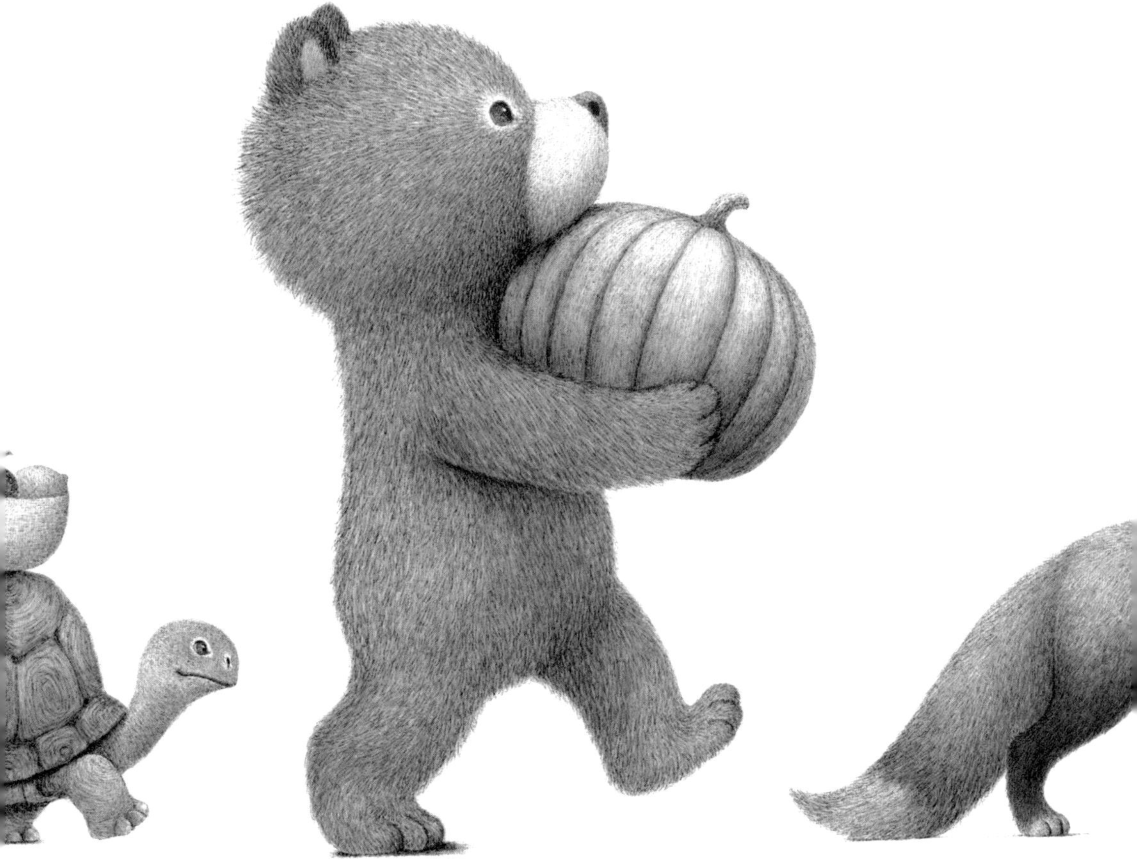

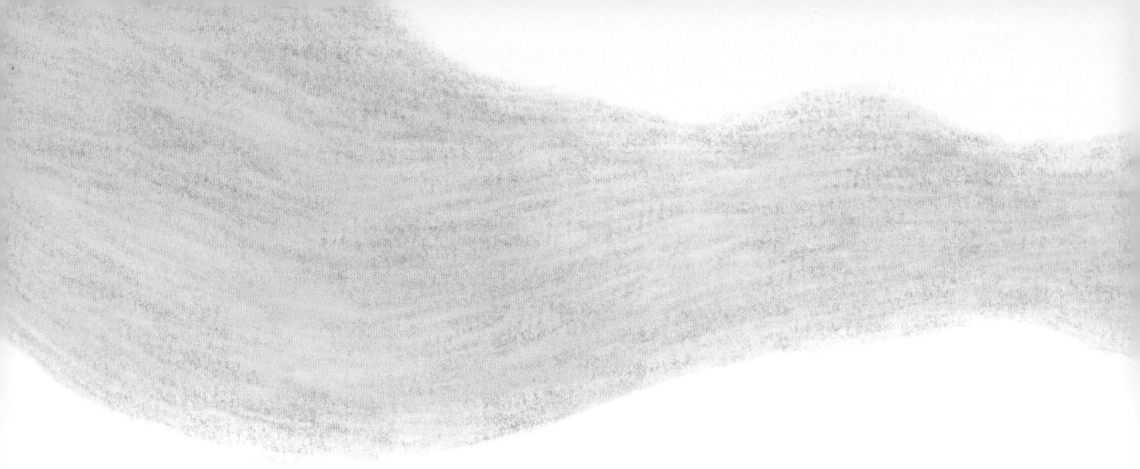

Get involved. Be there for someone else when they need you. When we all help, everyone benefits.

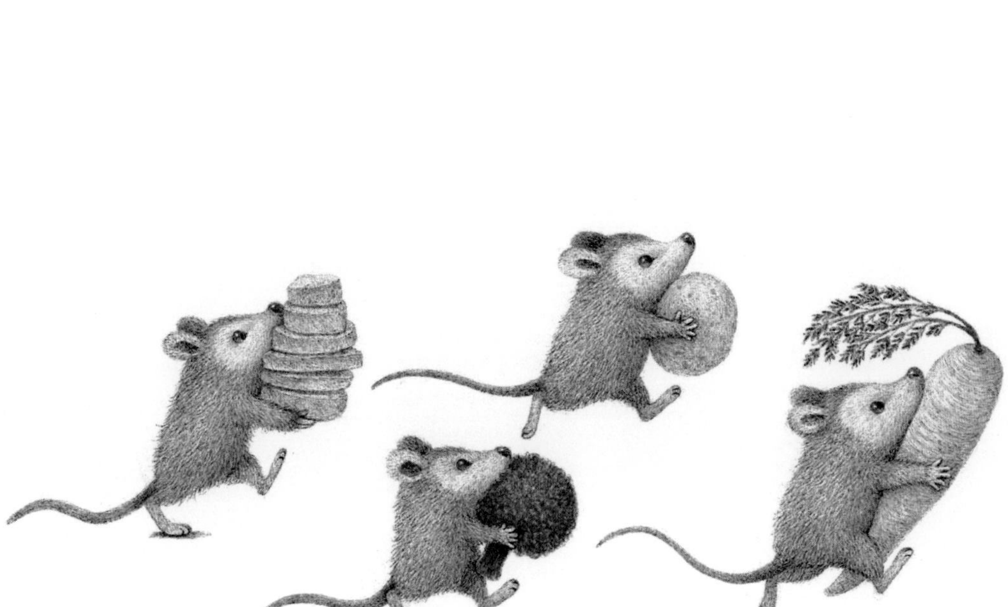

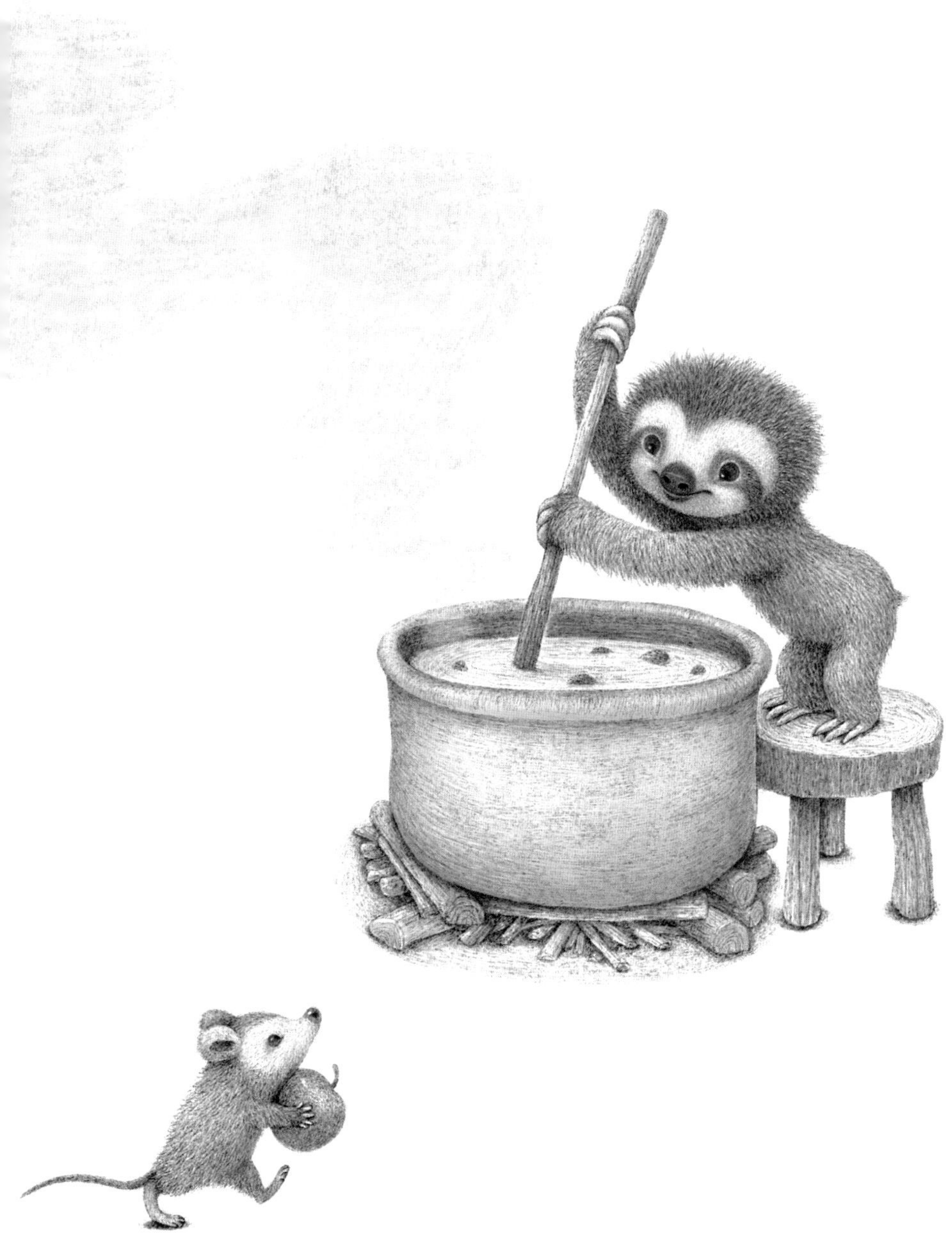

Do more of what gives your heart the feeling of bigness.

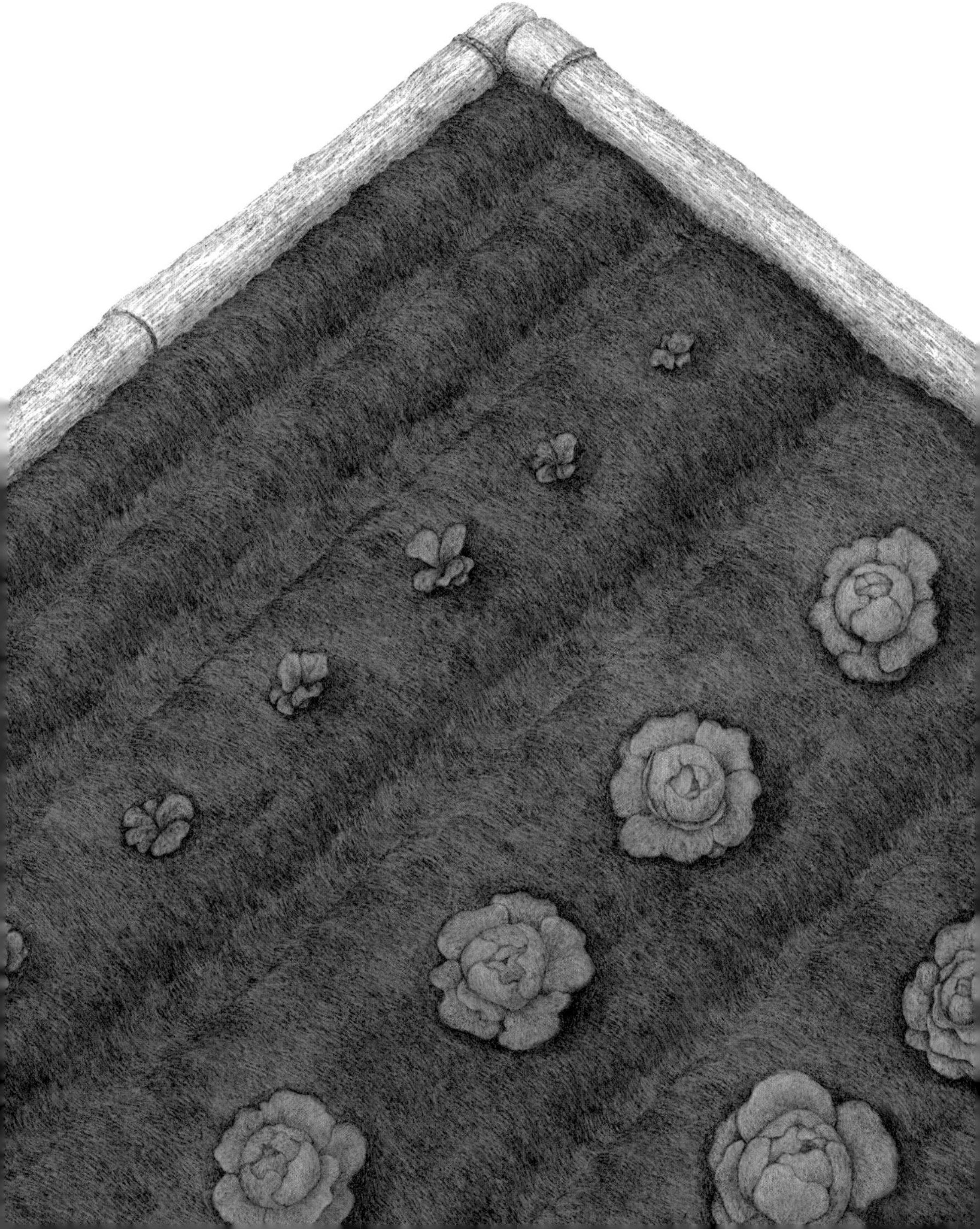

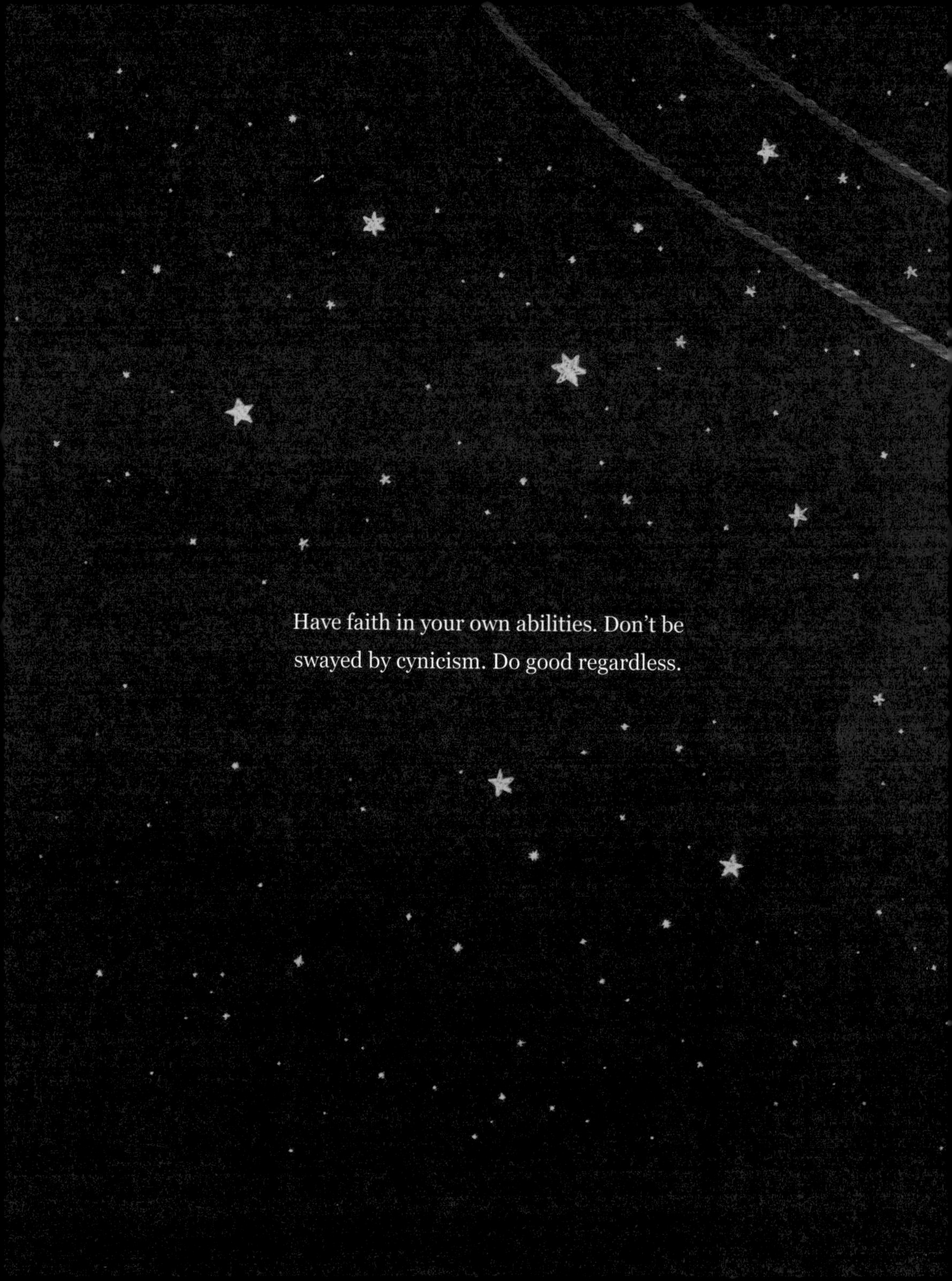

Have faith in your own abilities. Don't be swayed by cynicism. Do good regardless.

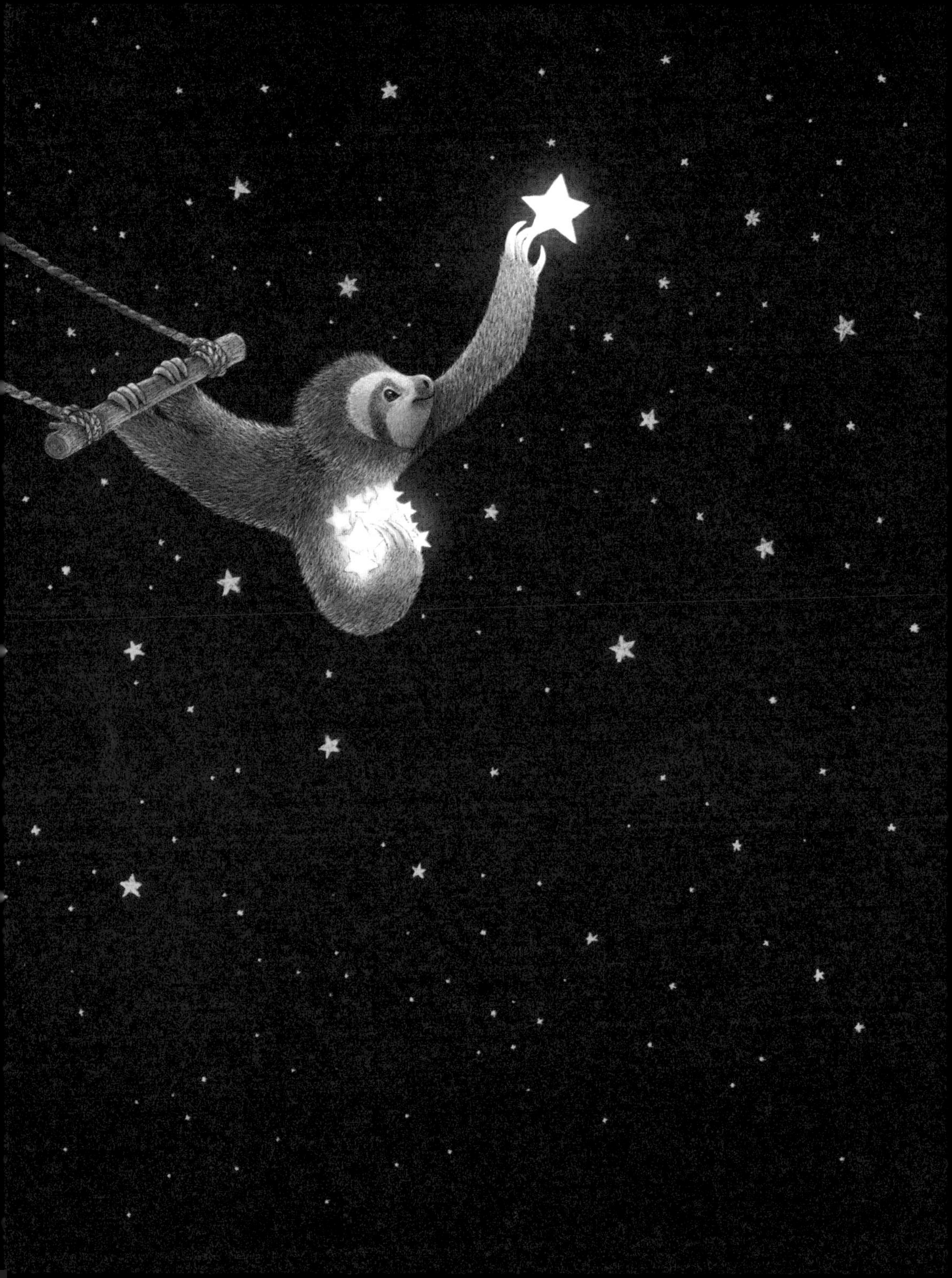

Embrace who you are.
Recognize *yourself* as a friend.

Be part of something you believe in.
Challenge your fears and insecurities that
try to convince you that you don't matter.

Know that you matter. There is no place in
the world more important than where you are.
And while none of us can be everything to everyone,
each of us can be something to someone.

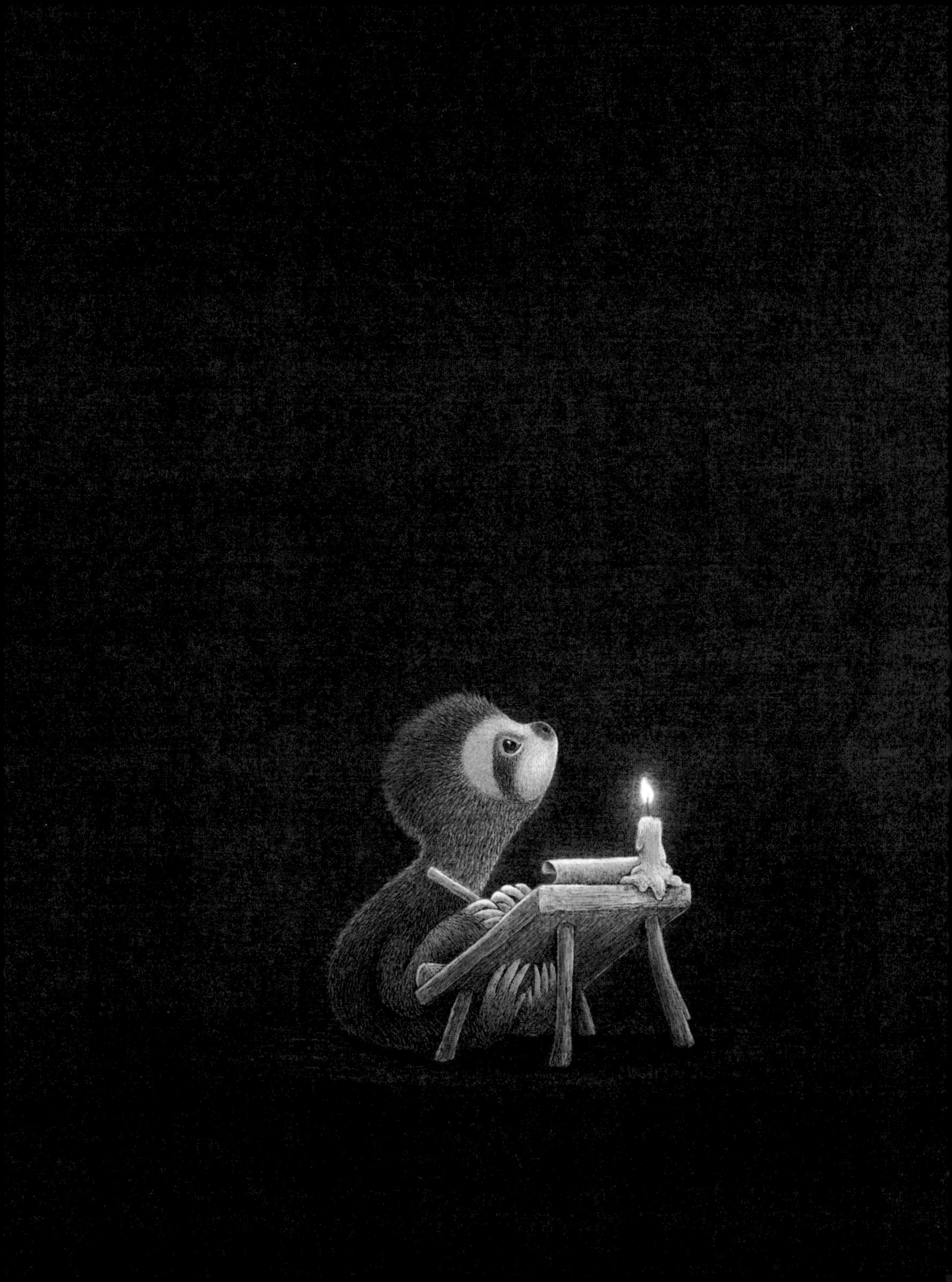

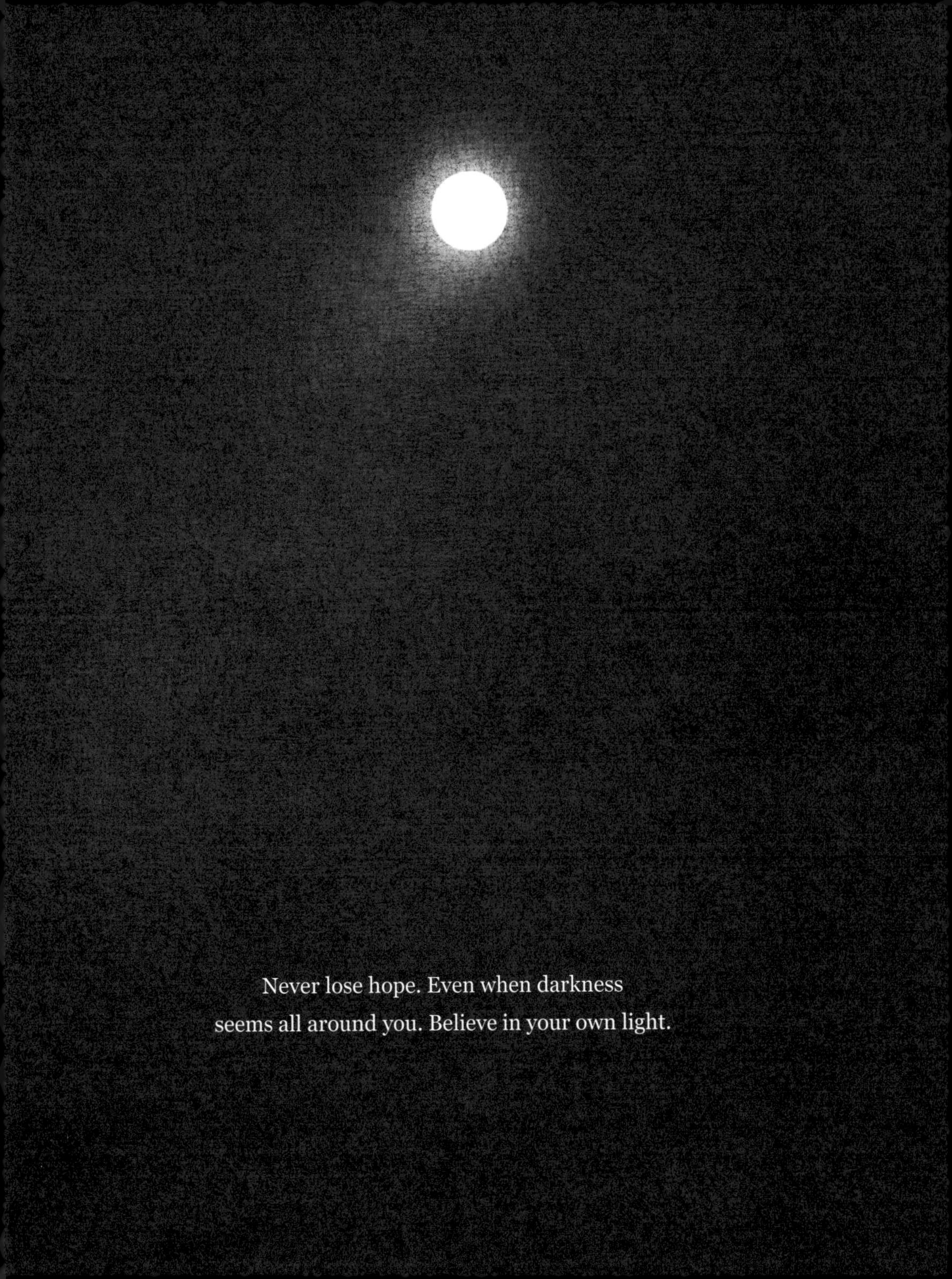

Never lose hope. Even when darkness
seems all around you. Believe in your own light.

Be patient with your progress. Sometimes it can take
a little *extra* to see the extraordinary in the ordinary:
extra caring, *extra* focus, *extra* love.

Everyone struggles. Everyone doubts.
Gently accept the messy, imperfect parts of you,
even if you wish they were different.

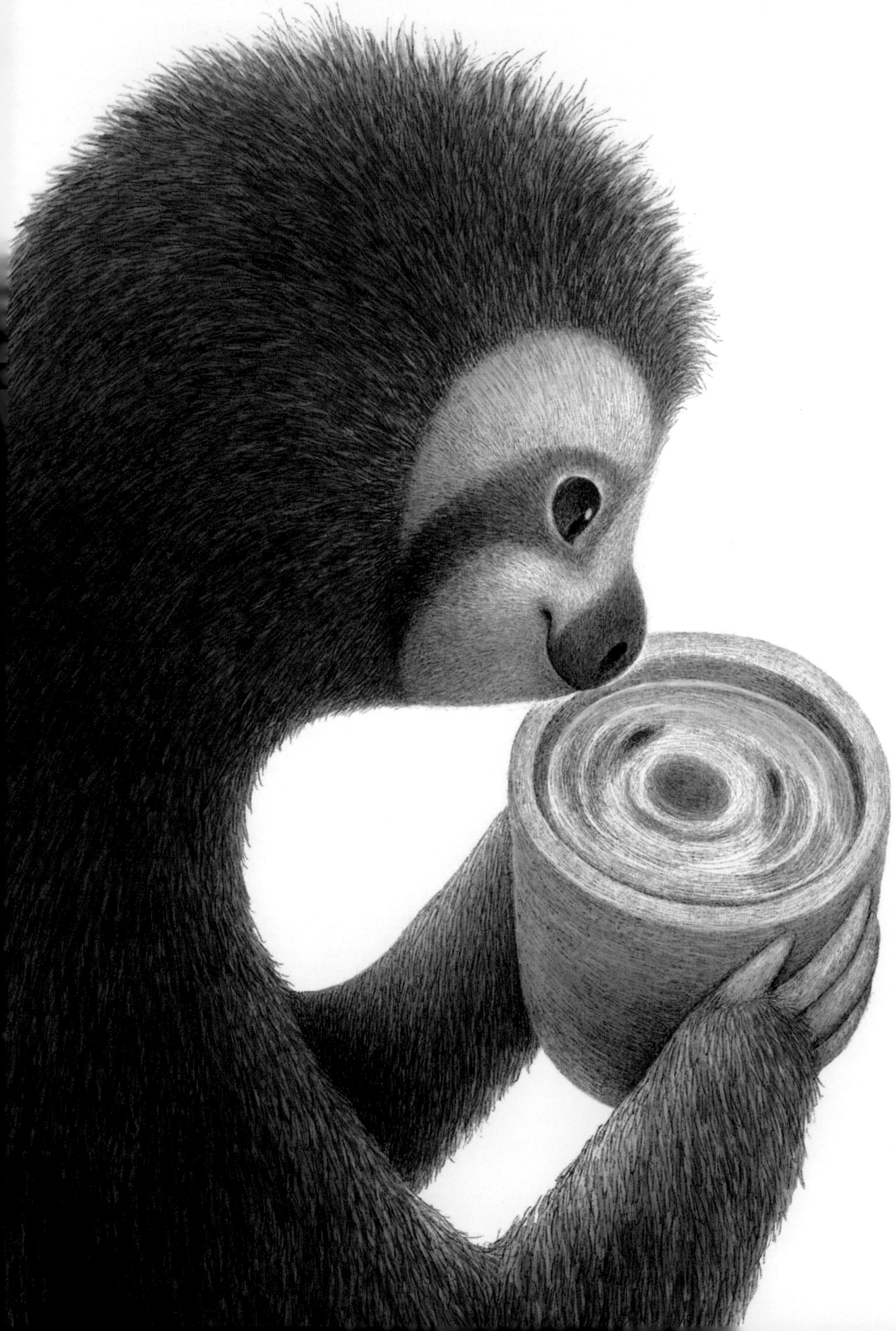

Appreciate what makes you *you*. When was the last time you looked at yourself and said, "I love you"?

Think like you love yourself. Speak like you love yourself.
How you talk to yourself is as important as
the food you eat and the air you breathe.

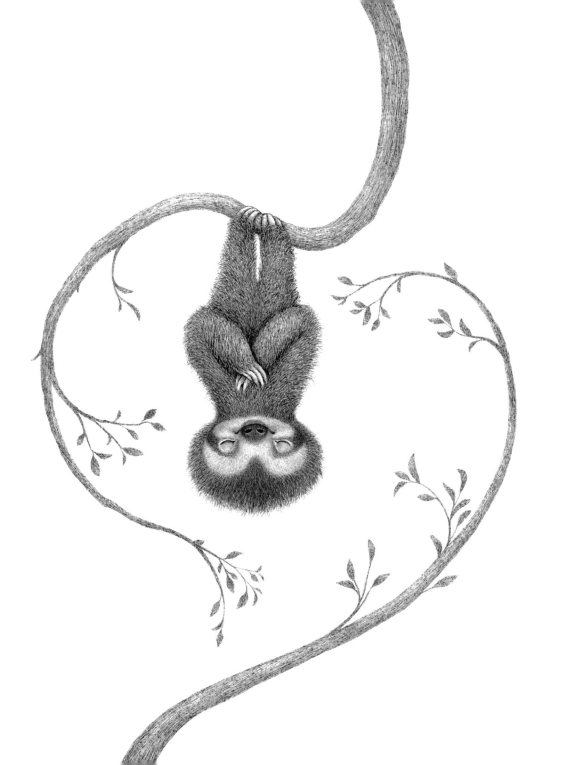

Be kind to yourself. In those moments when
you feel small and insignificant, when everything seems difficult,
and nothing is going right... be especially kind to yourself.

Make time for your well-being. Make time for what restores and renews you.
Calm and relaxation begin in the mind, then move through the body.

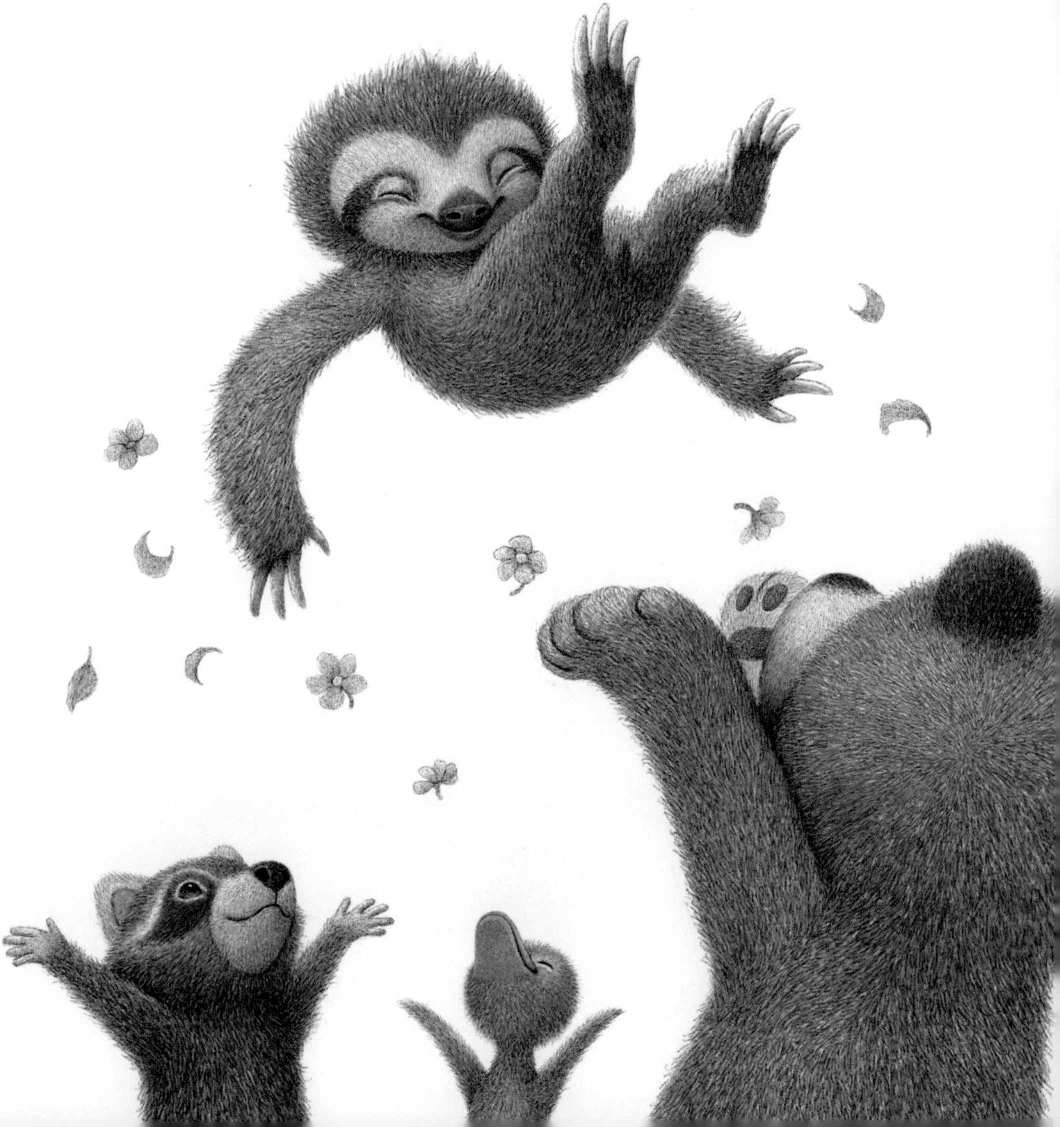

Surround yourself with people who care about you.

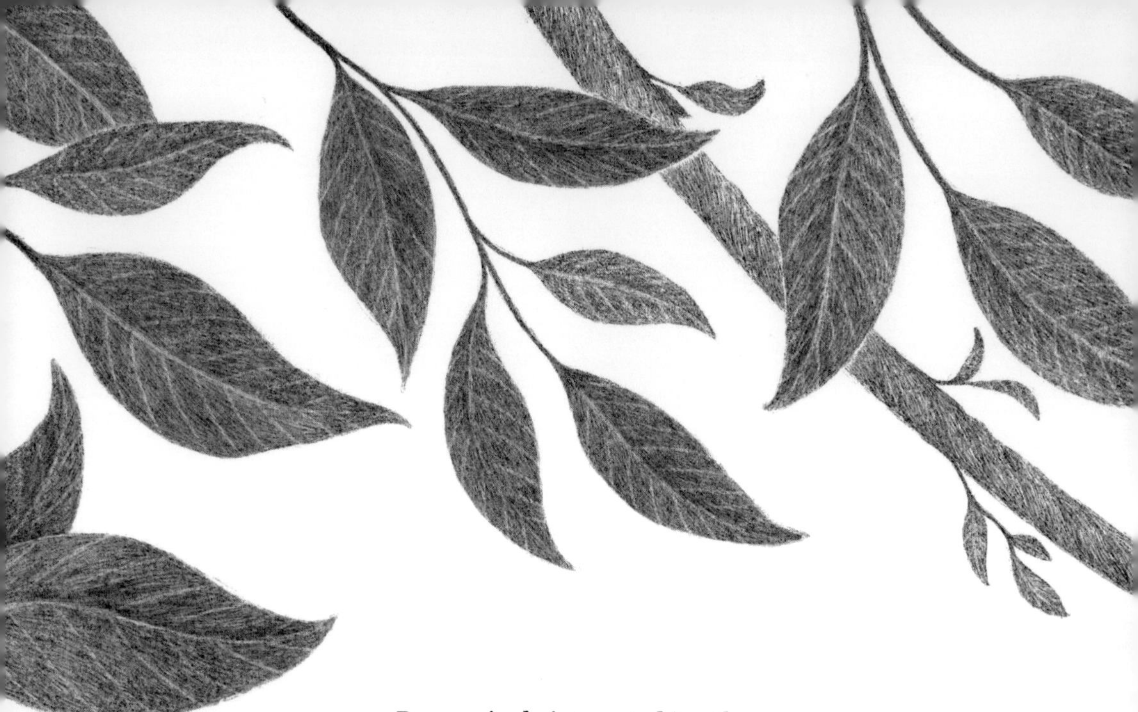

Be genuinely interested in others.

Help someone feel valued, cared for, and important.

Listening is a form of curiosity. Listening is an act of love.

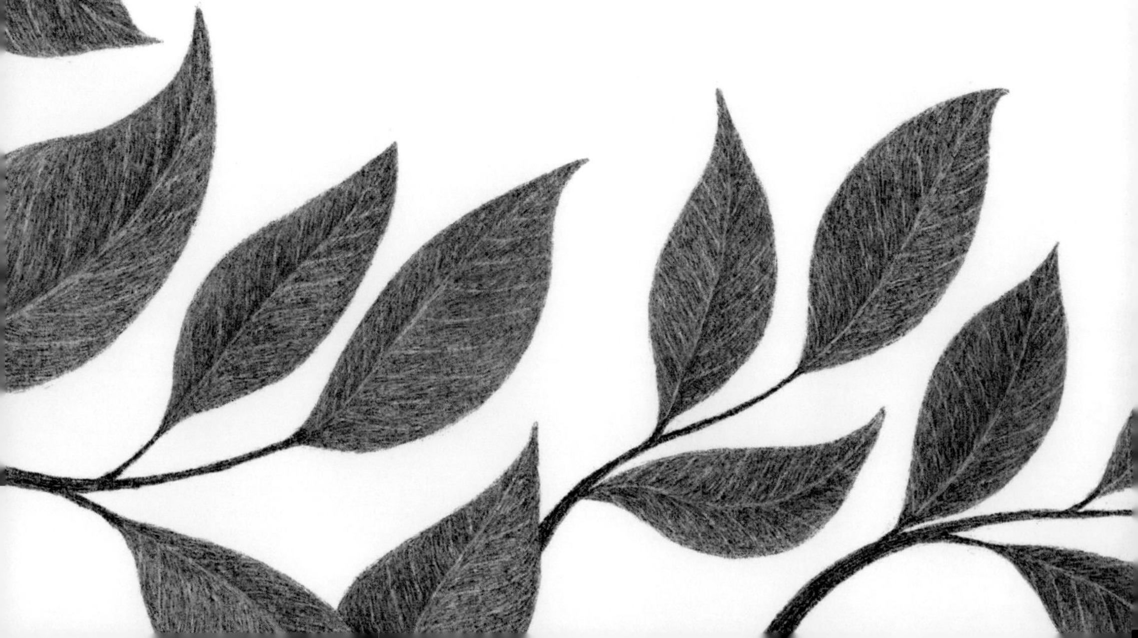

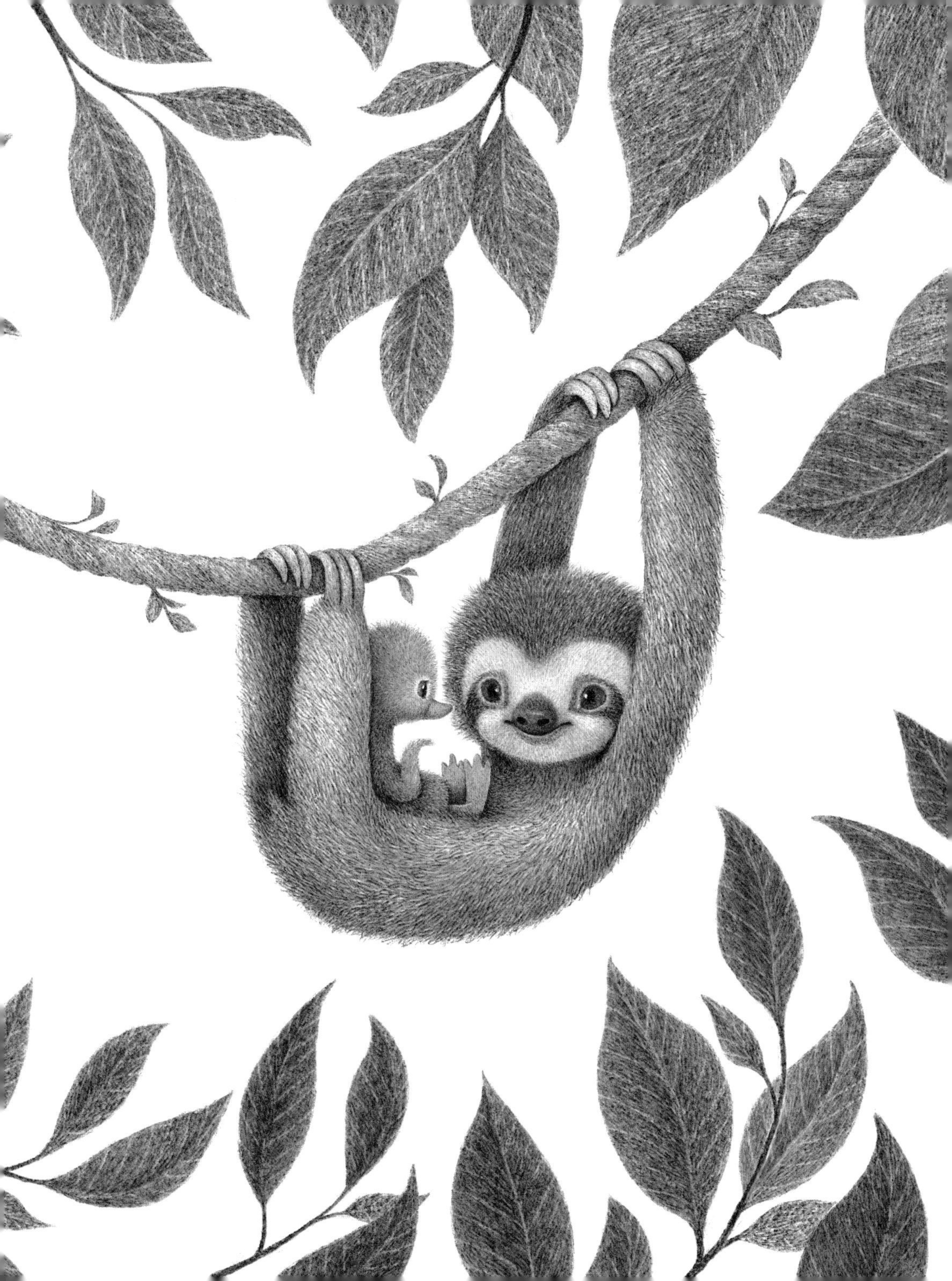

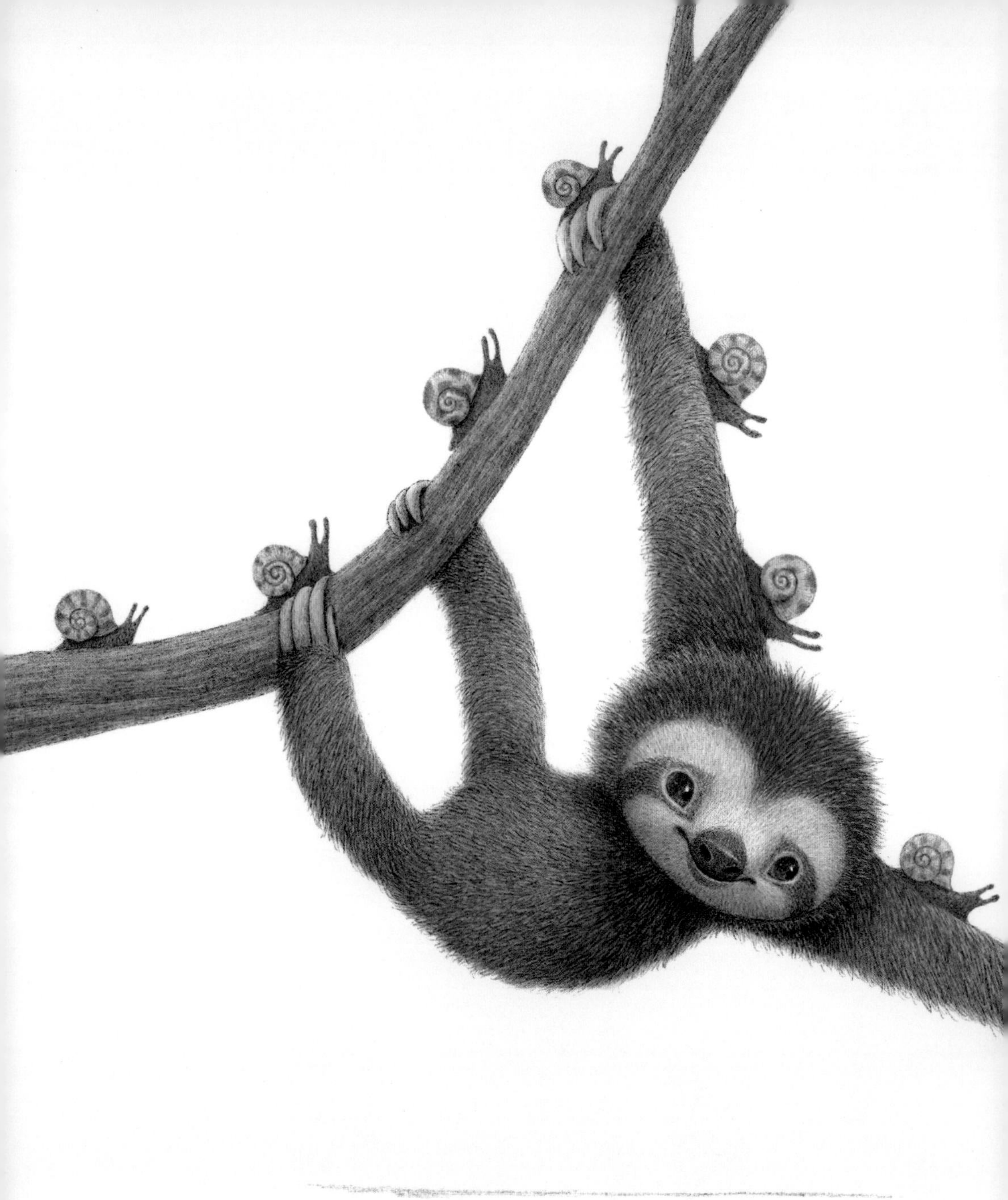

Extend yourself. Reach out. Make the effort.
You never know when a small gesture could have a big impact.

Love those you love. None of us are here forever.
Moments live on through our memories, and some
hugs stay with us long after we have let go.

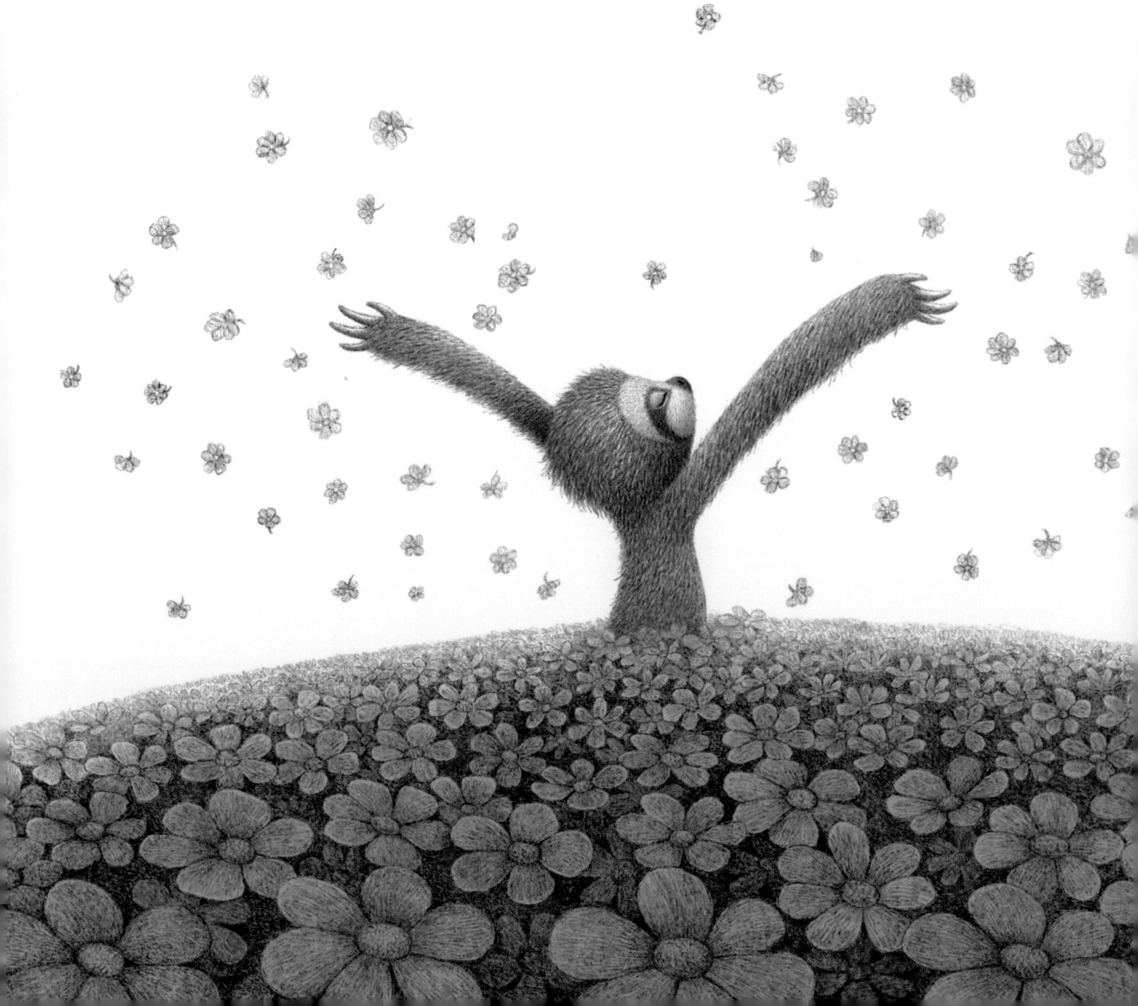

Make the most of your life. Each heartbeat brings with it
the chance to live more fully and to make the world a little kinder.

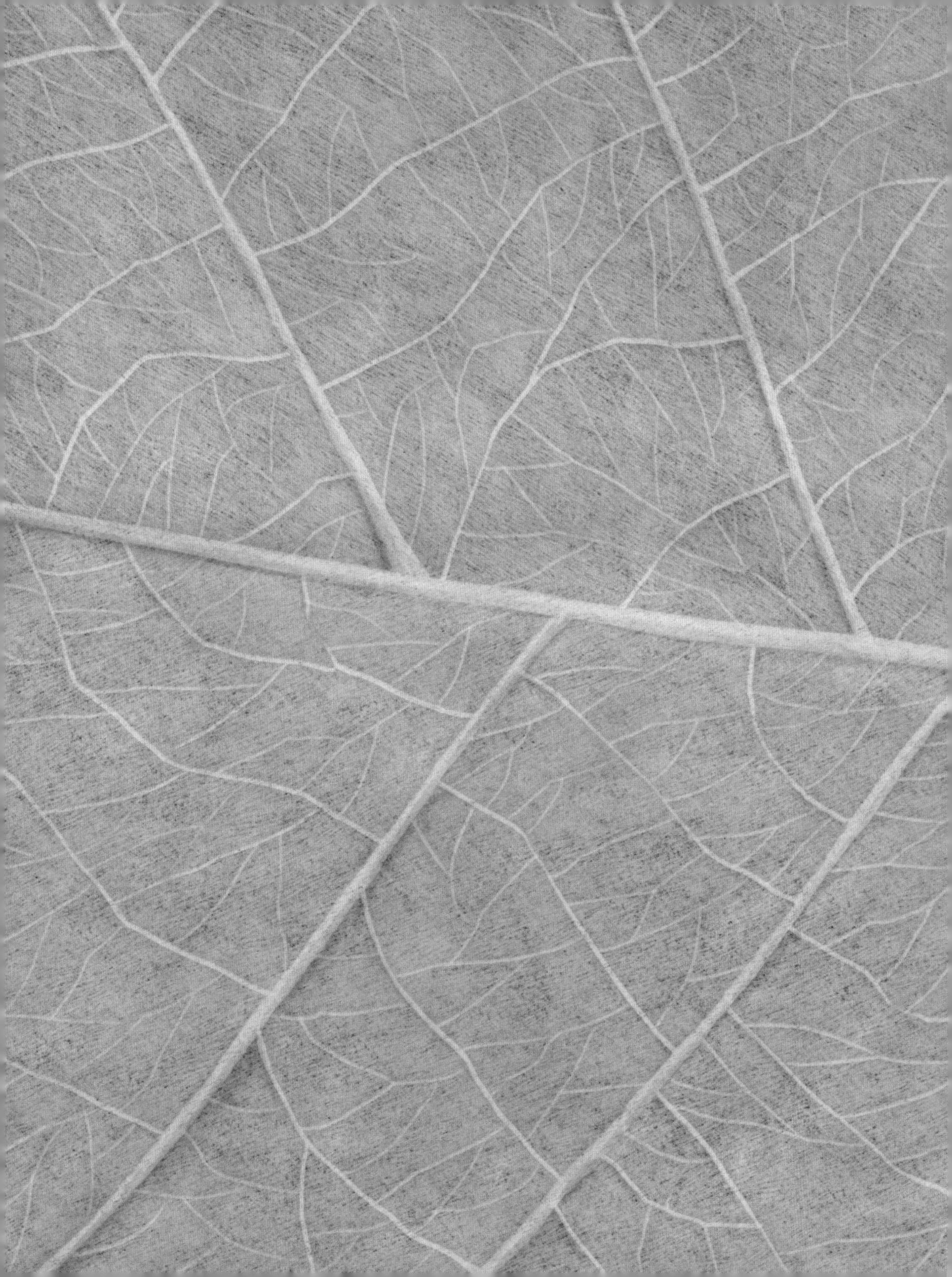